FIREARMS TRAINING INSTITUTE

Practice Guide
Uzi Submachine Gun

All inquiries should be addressed to:
Front Sight Firearms Training Institute
P. O. Box 2619
Aptos, CA 95001
(800) 987-7719

ISBN 0-9711266-4-X

Design and Editing by: Chuck Burnett and J. Scott Hoerner
Photography and Captions by: Chuck Burnett and Dennis Bower
Demonstrations by: Brad Ackman

Contents

Part Three

Disclaimer

This Practice Guide is not intended as a substitute for the safe and professional instruction provided in Front Sight's Uzi Submachine Gun Course.

THIS IS NOT A TRAINING MANUAL. FRONT SIGHT STRONGLY ADVISES YOU AGAINST PRACTICING THE TECHNIQUES IN THIS PRACTICE GUIDE UNLESS YOU HAVE COMPLETED THE FOUR DAY UZI COURSE AT FRONT SIGHT.

Front Sight assumes no liability for any damages or negligence that may occur through the use of this Practice Guide.

Students wishing to pursue training should contact Front Sight at (800) 989-7719 or www.frontsight.com.

Front Sight recommends that all procedures and techniques mentioned in this guide be performed at a proper firing range under carefully controlled conditions. By using this guide, the reader accepts the responsibility for any and all accidents, damage or injuries that might occur.

PART ONE

In this section:

The Purpose of This Practice Guide

At Front Sight, our goal is to make you as good as we possibly can during the time you spend with us. That, however, is only part of the process to gaining lasting skills in gun-handling, marksmanship, and tactics, and establishing a combat mindset. When you leave Front Sight, it becomes your responsibility to practice the techniques you learned during your course at Front Sight.

To assist you in your continued practice, we have created this guide. It reviews many of the techniques taught in the 4-Day Uzi Course. This guide is more than just a "dry practice" review. Many of the described techniques, such as malfunctions and reloads, involve a loaded weapon. Such techniques cannot be practiced safely during dry practice and must be practiced only at a proper firing range under carefully controlled "live-fire" conditions.

Practice diligently; practice often; and by all means — practice CORRECTLY!

The Four Universal Firearms Safety Rules

Rule 1: Treat every weapon as if it were loaded.

Dry practice means practicing with an unloaded weapon to polish the skills and techniques learned on the range. Even during dry practice, treat the weapon with the same respect as a loaded weapon. That respect, or mindset, generally prevents any negligent discharge that might otherwise occur. A negligent discharge means firing a round that you didn't anticipate firing.

Rule 2: Never let the muzzle cover anything you are not willing to destroy.

Usually, if you violate Rule 2 what you end up covering is yourself. You end up covering your hand, your leg, or some other body part. You need to be what we call "muzzle conscious." Know where that muzzle is pointing all the time and never point it at anything you do not intend to shoot.

Rule 3: Keep your finger off the trigger until you're ready to fire.

When you are pointed in at your target and have made the decision to shoot, ONLY THEN is your finger on the trigger. Any other time the trigger finger is resting on the reference point.

Rule 4: Be sure of your target and what's inline with your target.

On the shooting range your target is generally a flat sheet of paper. No one is in the foreground because everyone is on the same firing line. There is nothing behind the target except a large berm to absorb the impact of the rounds. On the street, Rule 4 is significantly more complicated. Several questions need to be answered. First, are you about to shoot the correct individual? If the answer is yes, then is someone going to step in front of your sights? And finally, if you press the trigger and that round over penetrates right through your adversary and continues downrange, what's it going to strike downrange? It goes without saying that once you have fired that shot you cannot alter it's course and you certainly can't get it back. You need to be absolutely certain of Rule 4 before you press the trigger.

The Five Levels of Competence

Intentionally Incompetent: Believe it or not, there are those who own and carry firearms that clearly know of their incompetence, but lack even the slightest bit of courage or motivation to improve their skills. The **II** avoids training out of laziness and fear of further exposing his incompetence to others. Graveyards are filled with the **II**. Sadly, the **II** often take those who count on them most — partners, family, and team members — to the grave with him. Unfortunately, the **II** cannot be helped to any substantial degree due to his lack of motivation to retain any training. Time wasted by coddling the **II** is better spent on the student who wants to improve. Fortunately, we rarely see the **II** at Front Sight.

Unconsciously Incompetent: The **UI** does not know that he does not know. The **UI** represents approximately 95% of all gun owners and includes people, for example in the police and military, who carry a gun for a living. The **UI** is incompetent but does not know he is incompetent because he has had no training or poor training, and has not yet experienced a tactical situation, which would clearly demonstrate his inadequacies. Examples of the **UI** can be found everywhere. The police officer who boasts that he has never had to draw his pistol in 10 years of duty is a lucky **UI**. The officer who only practices shooting his weapon a few times per year in order to pass the mandatory range qualifications is **UI**. The gun owner who buys a gun and box of ammo, fires a few shots at the range and then places the gun in his closet, confident he can use it effectively to protect himself is **UI**. The hunter who only shoots once a year to sight-in his rifle before going hunting is **UI**. Military personnel who receive basic rifle training, but have not handled a weapon **with live ammunition** in over six months are **UI**. Unfortunately, the **UI** often learns of his ineptitude for the first time under the most extreme stress situations. When the flag flies, the **UI's** first lesson may be his last.

Consciously Incompetent: If the **UI** survives his first lesson, and is smart enough to place the blame on the man in the mirror, the **UI** automatically graduates to the level of **CI**. The **CI** now knows he does not know and seeks help in acquiring the proper skills in the use of his weapon. The **CI** is a motivated student of weaponscraft. Although the **CI** is still operating at a level of incompetence, the **CI** recognizes his faults and in doing so can focus his efforts toward reaching a level of competency.

Consciously Competent: With proper training and practice, the **CI** develops into the **CC**. The length of time needed to develop from **CI** to **CC** is directly related to the quality of the training and the motivation of the student. The **CC** is able to manipulate his weapon and clear malfunctions in a safe and efficient manner. The **CC** understands the principles of marksmanship, shot placement and ammunition management. Quick assumption of field positions and the use of cover are familiar concepts to the **CC**. The **CC** has adopted the combat mind set as his own. As the level indicates, the **CC** is very quick and competent, but must constantly think about what he is doing. Every decision and action occurs as a result of an intricate thought process and has not yet reached a reflex response level. The **CC** will respond effectively to most stress situations that do not require split second decisions or actions.

Unconsciously Competent: As the fifth and ultimate level of competence implies, the **UC** has programmed his mind and body after thousands of repetitions to react in a fraction of a second with consistent responses that require no perceivable thought process. The **UC** functions flawlessly even under stressful situations because the **UC's** extensive training overrides his conscious thought process. As you can imagine, the **UC** is not common in today's society. This sad fact is due more to lack of proper training than to lack of motivation. Here are a few examples of the **UC in action**. In the heat of a gun battle, a pistolero hears a "click" as his hammer falls on a defective round. He reflexively taps the magazine, rack-flips the action and delivers two rounds into his adversary's chest without consciously recognizing that his gun had malfunctioned. Upon sighting a trophy, a hunter slings up as he drops into a steady sitting position. He fires, manipulates the bolt on recoil — without the rifle leaving his shoulder or his eyes leaving the game — producing a one-shot kill and he does it all in less time than it takes to read this sentence. The combat shotgunner, confronted with a rapidly deteriorating hostage situation at 10 yards, immediately aims his front sight at the outside ear of the gunman, then confidently delivers half of the shotgun's pattern to the gunman's head.

At Front Sight we take motivated people, conscious of their inadequacies or not, and develop their minds and bodies to a level of competence that transcends 95% of the people who carry firearms for a living. For those who are already competent, Front Sight will challenge your abilities and elevate your competence to the unconscious plane.

Dry Practice Procedures

by Brad Ackman, Operations Manager
Front Sight Firearms Training Institute

Strictly adhering to the procedures here will allow you to safely practice with your weapon when you leave the range.

A few definitions are needed for clarity:

Dry Practice:
Describes a practice session or exercise not involving ammunition. The weapon is completely unloaded. Note that we do not use the term "dry fire" as you cannot fire an unloaded weapon and when calling out a range command we do not want any confusion between dry practice and firing the weapon.

Live Fire:
Describes a practice session or exercise using ammunition. **The weapon is loaded.**

Negligent Discharge:
The act of firing the weapon unintentionally.

Notice that the words "accident" and "accidental discharge" have been purposely avoided because they imply a sense of chance or lack of control. A weapons fires only when the handler presses the trigger -- there is no element of chance involved. In our many years associated with weapons, we have never seen a gun of any kind fire by itself. The handler may not intend to fire a round, but he is responsible for it regardless of his intentions. The term "negligent discharge" more accurately places the responsibility where it belongs.

We are well advised to practice the skills we learned on the range. You cannot significantly improve your shooting skills through additional shooting and often the more you shoot, the worse you shoot. Your skill with firearms is maintained and improved through **CORRECT DRY PRACTICE.** The importance of dry practice cannot be overstated.

Homes, apartments, and hotels are clearly poor places for a bullet to unintentionally escape from the muzzle, yet because of convenience, these are the places we most commonly dry practice. The following system will allow you to safely conduct dry practice anywhere.

The three main elements of safe dry practice are:
- Proper mind set
- Control of your environment, and
- Separation from ammunition

Proper Mind Set: Because safety lies between the ears and not with mechanical devices, proper mindset is crucial to safe dry practice. Realize that handling weapons can be disastrous if the handler's attention is elsewhere. Dry practice must be conducted in a structured, serious fashion. Often as familiarity increases, so does complacency. This gives rise to many seasoned shooters having negligent discharges. Some people believe that if you handle weapons long enough you will eventually have a negligent discharge. We strongly disagree. There is no reason, other than negligence, that you will unintentionally fire a round. If you treat dry practice with the respect it demands, you will never feel the helpless agony associated with tracing the path of the round that you did not want to fire or have to utter the hollow excuse, "I didn't mean to shoot."

Control of Your Environment: For safe dry practice you must have control of your immediate environment so you can eliminate all possible distractions. If you don't have control of your environment, don't dry practice until you do.

In preparation for dry practice:
- Turn off the television and stereo
- Take the telephone off the hook
- Close the drapes
- Send the family on an errand

15

This distraction-free environment will help result in safe and productive practice. Part of your practice environment is obviously the target.

- Construct a target specifically for dry practice. The target should be used for dry practice only and should be removed immediately when you have finished practicing. Don't use part of the building (doors, mirrors, or light switches) or its furnishings (televisions, pictures, computers) because these items may tempt you to practice your presentation "just one more time" after you have quit your dry practice session and have holstered the weapon. This sounds unbelievable, but is the most common reason for negligent discharges.

- Select a simple target, such as a piece of white paper cut to a desired size. If you want to simulate shooting at longer distances within the confines of your home, reduce the size of the target. For added precaution, tape your target to something capable of stopping, or at least slowing, a bullet. A brick or cinder block wall is ideal.

- At the conclusion of the practice session, remove the target to avoid the "just one more time" syndrome described above. Some people advocate dry practicing in conjunction with watching television as the characters in the program serve as targets and the scene change is your start signal. This is bad business (except for the television repair man) because the person practicing tends to shift his attention to the television, thereby diluting his concentration and losing control of his immediate environment. The television also remains as a tempting target after the dry practice session is over. Many televisions have been destroyed in this process. Besides, the thin veneers of glass and plastic that comprise a television do not make a good bullet stop.

Separation from Ammunition: Physical separation from your ammunition supply is mandatory to ensure a safe dry practice session. Unload your weapon AND yourself. This includes

- The chamber
- All magazines and speed loaders
- Ammunition carrying devices such as butt cuffs on long guns
- Your pockets

Place all the ammunition in a container such as an ammo can or range bag and put it in another room, away from where you will be dry practicing. You will remain in one room only while dry practicing, so you will effectively be separated from your ammunition supply.

Questions:

1. What about keeping ammunition in the magazines so the have the proper weight, feel, and function for reloading or malfunction clearing practice?

   ABSOLUTELY NOT. At some point you will end up with a round in the chamber. The muscle memory you program through dry practice with an empty magazine will be no different than using a full magazine.

2. What about using snap caps or similar devices to protect the weapon from the hammer falling on an empty chamber repeatedly?

   This too is a poor idea because the habit of placing something in the chamber prior to dry practice will eventually lead to a negligent discharge. It is also likely that your snap caps can find their way into your live ammunition and result in a *click* when you wanted a *bang*! This can be hazardous to your health as well. In terms of damage to your weapon, with the exception of rim-fire handguns and rifles, dry practice is not detrimental to a modern weapon.

Dry Practice Checklist

- Set a realistic dry practice goal before you start. A long practice session is not necessarily better because quality, not quantity, is the goal.
- Establish the proper mind set for dry practice.
- Establish and maintain control of your dry practice environment to eliminate all possible distractions.
- **UNLOAD THE WEAPON AND YOURSELF** and place the ammunition in another room.
- Chamber check the weapon to verify that it is unloaded and say, "The weapon is unloaded and I am ready for dry practice."
- Select an appropriate sized target and place it on a solid surface capable of stopping a bullet.
- Chamber check the weapon again and then begin dry practice.
- Terminate the dry practice session before significant physical and mental fatigue set in.
- Remove the dry practice target immediately upon finishing the dry practice session.
- Return the weapon to fighting mode — loaded and placed in its usual location such as a holster, fanny pack, briefcase, or nightstand.
- Say aloud, "The weapon is loaded and dry practice is over."

PART TWO

In this section:

Uzi Discussion

The Uzi submachine gun was designed by Uziel Gal in the late 1940s for the Israeli army.

It is a magazine fed, blowback operated, select-fire submachine gun which fires from the open bolt.

The standard 9mmUzi fires at a rate of 600 rounds per minute on full auto. This moderate cyclic rate makes it easy to modulate the trigger to deliver single shots or controlled bursts of two to three rounds per trigger press.

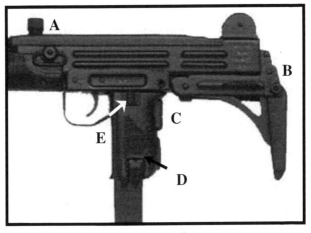

A- Charging handle
B– Folding stock
C– Grip Safety
D– Magazine release
E– Selector switch

A three position selector switch on the left side of the weapon is used to select safety on, semi-automatic, or full automatic operation.

The Uzi is equipped with a grip safety to prevent the gun from firing without a full firing grip. This feature can induce malfunctions if the firing grip is relaxed during the firing cycle.

Reference Point for the Trigger Finger

The trigger finger should be off the trigger and rest along the frame of the weapon when not firing.

Thumb is staged on safety.

Clearing the Uzi

Note: Locking the bolt to the rear should always be the **first** step of manipulating an open-bolt weapon like the Uzi. This insures that the firing mechanism is holding the bolt and that it will not slip forward and slam fire a round.

Lock the bolt to the rear by grasping the charging handle and pull it to the rear as far as possible.

Let the charging handle run forward.

Push the magazine release to remove the magazine.

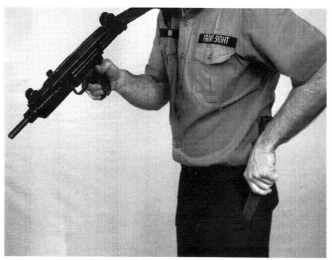

Stow the magazine in a pocket or pouch.

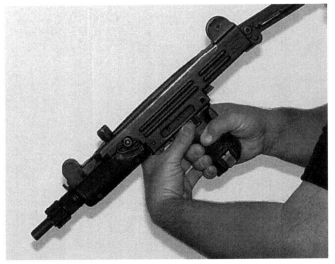

Engage the safety by sliding the selector switch to the rear (S) position.

Verify that the chamber is clear by looking and feeling with the tip of a finger

24

Double check that the magazine has been removed by inserting a finger in the magazine well.

The Uzi is now cleared.

Uzi Manipulation for Left-handed Shooters

Left handed shooters use the tip or ball of the trigger finger to push the selector switch forward from "Safe" to the firing position. The safety can be re-engaged with either hand.

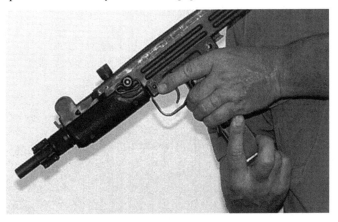

The magazine release is depressed by the support hand index finger.

Loading the Uzi

Begin the loading process by first clearing the gun.
Lock the bolt to the rear by grasping the charging handle and
pull it to the rear as far as possible.

Remove the magazine or verify that that there is none in
place.

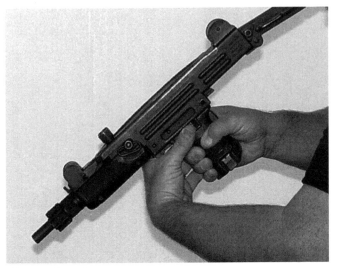

Engage the safety.

Verify that the chamber is clear by looking and feeling with
the tip of a finger

Double check that the magazine well is clear.

Index a magazine by grasping it below the indexing tabs with the cartridges facing forward.

Insert the magazine into the magazine well until it locks in place. Tug on the magazine to insure that it is locked into the magazine well.

The Uzi is now loaded.

Unloading the Uzi

To unload use the basic clearing procedure. Lock the bolt to the rear by grasping the charging handle and pull it to the rear as far as possible. Let the charging handle run forward.

Push the magazine release to remove the magazine. Stow the magazine in a pocket or pouch.

Engage the safety.

Verify that the chamber is clear by looking and feeling with
the tip of a finger

Double check that the magazine has been removed by inserting a finger in the magazine well.

The Uzi is now cleared.

Grip and Stance

How the shooter holds the Uzi, the gun's placement in the
shoulder pocket and on the cheek, and the shooter's body
position or posture combine to form a shooting position.
Consistency and efficiency in the assumption of shooting
positions will facilitate speed and accuracy.

Shoulders are well forward of the hips in an aggressively
forward posture. The head is fairly upright. The toe of the
stock is placed high in the shoulder pocket to bring the sights
up to the eye. The stock is pulled tightly into the pocket by
the firing hand. The support hand grip on the fore end is neutral without back pressure. The cheek is pressed firmly into
the comb of the stock.

34

The body is bladed comfortably so that feet, knees, hips, and shoulders are aligned.

Rolling the elbows inward as though "wringing out a dish-rag" will tighten the upper torso and help manage recoil.

35

Mounting the Gun From the Ready Position

The **ready** position has the gun in the shoulder pocket with the muzzle depressed enough to allow a clear field of view. Shooter's trigger finger is straight, and the thumb is staged on the selector switch, ready to disengage the safety.

On the firing cue, safety comes off and gun pivots up to the cheek weld. Finger goes on the trigger as the sights come onto the target.

High Ready

The **high ready** position has the stock trapped between body and forearm with the muzzle angled upward just below the line of sight. "Eye, muzzle, target".

On the firing cue, safety comes off and gun pushes forward to clear the body and then pulls straight back into the pocket.

Field Ready

The **field ready** position has the gun angled down and across to the support side. "All day carry" with relaxed, upright posture. Note that the stock is roughly parallel with the forearm. *(Shown with M16 for illustration)*

On the firing cue, safety comes off and gun arcs up and forward to clear the body and then pulls straight back into the pocket.

After Action Drills

Once an opponent has been engaged and is not an immediate, shootable threat, perform after action drills to secure the environment. **Quick check** the immediate area for further threats, refocus on the primary adversary for a **final check** on him, then **scan** the surroundings in detail. Remember that the known, deadly threat in front of you takes precedence unless you are already aware of other threats. It is always advisable to move to cover or to an advantageous position during a fight, yet on the live fire range it is not safe to move to any great extent. **Safe dry practice is the venue to ingrain the habit of moving to cover.**

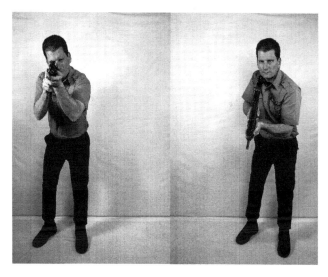

If your opponent is a deadly threat, shoot him until the threat stops! Once the threat has ceased, lower the weapon to assess the situation **while moving** to a position of cover or advantage. If you are not shooting, finger comes off the trigger.

While maintaining awareness of the downed opponent, **quick check** the immediate area for other threats. Turn the head only for brief "snapshots" and return to the primary threat.

The **final check** of the downed adversary may take seconds
or minutes. You may have to keep your attention on him
until police arrive or you can retreat. If your opponent is still
a potential threat, move to a position of advantage and use
quick checks to maintain awareness of your surroundings.
Reload and check your gun! When it is safe to do so,
perform a detailed <u>scan</u> of your environment, eyes and
muzzle aligned like the turret of a tank. Scan in vertical
bands, near to far, in a 360 degree circle.

Remember that, on the street, the entire after action sequence
is done from cover or a position of advantage. Do **not**
ingrain the habit of standing in the open while practicing
after action drills.

After Action Drills Summary

- **Finish the fight!**

  Don't take your attention off of an active, <u>known</u> threat to look for <u>potential</u> threats.

- **Move!**

  Don't be an exposed, static target. Move aggressively to a position of cover or advantage.

  Circle a downed opponent as you quick check to clear your surroundings if you need to.

  Escape if you can do so safely.

- **Fight off tunnel vision**

  Once the main threat is down, look around.

  Take a few slow, deep breaths.

- **Keep your gun running!**

  Reload your rifle at every opportunity.

  Chamber check or glance at your gun to make sure it's functional.

- **Check for injuries!**

  Check yourself for injuries that you may not have felt. Apply direct pressure to stop any serious bleeding.

- **Call for help!**

  Get police and medics on their way. Make sure that dispatch knows that you're the victim. Be very careful as the police arrive so they don't perceive you as a threat.

Tactical Reload

Remove the partially depleted magazine from the gun.

Retain the partial magazine by stowing it in a pocket.

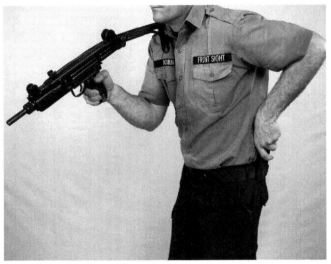

Index a fully loaded magazine.

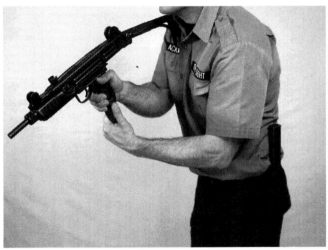

Insert the loaded magazine into the magazine well until it
locks in place. Verify proper seating with a tug.

The gun is now fully loaded

Three Secrets - Sight Alignment

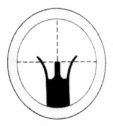

Sight Alignment is the relationship between the firing eye, rear sight and front sight. With ghost ring sights, correct Sight Alignment is when the *tip* of the front sight is centered both vertically and horizontally in the rear sight aperture.

Sight Picture

Sight Picture is placing correct Sight Alignment center mass on the target. The target and the rear sight should be out of focus, with a sharp, clear view of the tip of the front sight. In order to get this clear view of the front sight tip, the support eye should be closed. Correct Sight Alignment and Sight Picture are extremely critical the further away from the target you are. Slight errors in either that allow reasonable hits at close range will cause misses at greater distances.

Trigger Control

Trigger control is manipulating the trigger in such a manner that when the shot is fired, Sight Alignment and Sight Picture are not disturbed. The trigger press must be straight to the rear and consistent. Pressing the trigger is a physical skill; controlling the trigger is a mental skill.

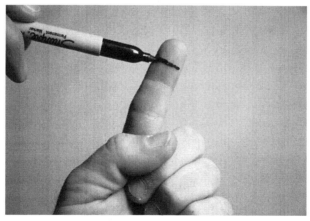

In order to control the trigger, the placement of the trigger finger needs to be consistent. Ideally, the center of the pad should be in contact with the trigger (above) in order to apply steady pressure straight to the rear.

The next element of trigger control is taking the slack out of the trigger. Slack is the initial rearward travel of the trigger before the internal components "engage" to fire the gun. Once the slack is taken up, apply a steady rearward pressure while keeping the sights aligned on target. Submachineguns are most effective when fired in short bursts of two to three rounds. To achieve this the trigger is modulated in a press-release action with the finger staying in contact with the trigger between bursts. With practice, the Uzi trigger can be modulated to fire a single shot or the entire magazine with a single controlled press-release of the trigger.

When first Dry Practicing presentation and the Three Secrets, it will be more beneficial to separate them. Practice presentations, being as consistent and as smooth as possible in mounting the gun, acquiring the sights, and placing the trigger finger on the trigger.

When working on trigger control, use a blank or neutral background to aim in at so all there is to look at are the sights. Watch the front sight carefully when manipulating the trigger. Any movement in the front sight when the hammer falls on the dry press indicates an error in trigger control.

Once there is no movement in the sights when the trigger is pressed, alternate presenting to the blank background and the dry practice target while pushing to go a little faster each time. If movement of the front sight begins to creep in during the dry press, slow down, or separate presentation from the Three Secrets again until the trigger control is back.

Tactical Sling Carry

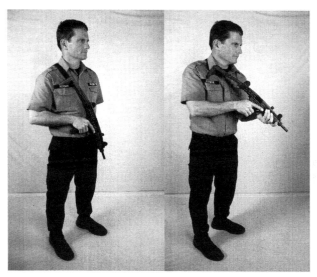

In Front Sight classes, the Uzi is often carried in a simple two point sling looped over the head and support arm.
To mount the gun, disengage the safety as you arc the gun forward and upward.

Pull the Uzi straight back into the shoulder pocket.

Malfunction Clearance

A **malfunction** is loosely defined as an interruption in the cycle of operation of the gun that can be remedied in the field quickly without the use of tools. In contrast, a **jam** is a stoppage that will require tools, disassembly, or even an armorer's services to clear it. If we experience a jammed gun mid-fight our options are retreat or transition to another weapon.

If our weapon malfunctions we first try to deal with it on a symptom specific basis, i.e. look at or feel the weapon to see what's wrong and then fix that specific problem. With practice, the physical clearance procedures should be ingrained to the point of being nearly reflexive. Once the malfunction is cleared, however, the decision to fire or not must be a **conscious decision**. Take care in your malfunction clearance practice not to ingrain a trigger press as the unthinking reflexive finale of the clearance process.

A serious malfunction or an empty gun may take you out of the fight for several seconds. Standing in place with your gun inoperative makes you an easy target. Since aggressive movement is seldom allowed during range practice, it is all too easy to ingrain the habit of standing still while managing your gun. Fight this trend by incorporating functional movement into your dry practice.

Transitioning to a backup weapon is a great option, if you have a backup weapon. Clubbing your adversary with the inoperative firearm may be necessary at close quarters.

If you have cleared a malfunction and not fired, **check the gun** to ensure that the malfunction was cleared.

Type One Malfunction: Failure to Fire

The symptom of a type one is a dry trigger press; a "click" instead of a "bang" as the bolt slams forward without firing.

Briskly tap the base of the magazine with the base of the support side palm and tug on the magazine to verify that it is locked in place.

51

Simultaneously run the bolt to the rear and roll the gun 90 degrees to the ejection port side. "Rack-Flip"

Make the decision to fire or not. Notice that the gun stays high throughout the procedure.

Type Two Malfunction: Failure to Eject

The initial symptom is a "dead" trigger, which does not give enough information.

Roll the gun ejection port up so you can see the chamber. A shell casing protruding from the ejection port indicates a failure to eject.

"Tap - Tug" on the magazine.

Visual focus is back on the threat as you "Rack-flip".
Make the decision to fire or not.

54

Type Three Malfunctions: Failure to Extract

A type three malfunction, or failure to extract, occurs when the casing in the chamber is not extracted as the bolt moves rearward. As the gun cycles, a live round is released onto the carrier and driven into the back of the stuck casing. On occasion, a live round will be stuck in the chamber with another round lodged behind it. This can be caused by a dirty or corroded chamber or shell, a weak or failed extractor, or an overloaded cartridge that over expanded when fired.

Whatever the cause, a type three malfunction may actually be a jam requiring that the stuck casing be driven or pried out of the chamber. The goal of our reflexive type three clearance procedure is to rapidly clear the chamber **or** quickly recognize a jam so we can take other actions.

The initial symptom is a "dead" trigger, which does not give enough information.

55

Start moving to cover!
Roll the gun ejection port up so you can see the chamber. A live round is stacked shell lodged in the chamber. "Brass low" in the ejection port.

Simultaneously run the bolt to the rear and roll the gun 90 degrees to the ejection port side. "Rack-Flip"

Strip the magazine out and drop it, unless it is your only magazine. In that case, retain the magazine by tucking it under the firing side arm.

Point in at the threat or in a safe direction and press the trigger to close the bolt.

The gun will fire if a live round is stuck in the chamber!

57

Run the bolt to the rear.

Insert a loaded magazine.

58

Make the decision to fire or not.

Emergency Reload

The first symptom of an empty gun is a dry trigger press; a "click" instead of a "bang" as the bolt slams forward without firing. This is a type one malfunction.

Briskly tap the base of the magazine with the base of the support side palm and tug on the magazine to verify that it is locked in place.

Simultaneously run the bolt to the rear and roll the gun 90
degrees to the ejection port side. "Rack-Flip"

Another "click" as you attempt to fire

Start moving to cover as you lock the bolt to the rear.

Remove the empty magazine and drop it.

Insert a loaded magazine and tug to verify that it is locked in position.

Make the decision to fire or not.

Supported Positions

Supported firing positions are used when a more stable firing platform is needed than the offhand position can provide, or when you need to conform to cover or concealment.

When choosing a supported position, keep in mind that you will still need to be able to see your target. Also be mindful of how long it will take to assume a position, and to get out of it in order to move, if you need to.

The supported positions discussed are under ideal circumstances, providing maximum bone support and muscle relaxation. When applied in the field, the positions will probably need to be modified to fit the terrain and the situation. Do what is necessary to get as stable as possible and get the hit!

Kneeling Position

Take a short step towards the target with the support foot, pointing it directly at the target. Safety comes off but finger is off and away from the trigger.

Ease the firing side knee to the ground. Support arm triceps braces on support knee. Note that shoulders are forward of hips for recoil control. Try to sit directly on the firing side foot.

Elbow drops to outside of knee for after action drills. Tactical reload should be done as soon as possible.

Shift your weight to the forward foot and recover to standing. Remember to keep scanning as you rise.

Sitting Position

Support foot steps across firing foot and then slightly rearward.

Lean torso forward and collapse straight down. Brace the triceps on your knees.

Open legged sitting position is most useful on uneven terrain.

The cross ankle sitting position with the upper body
stretched out over the extended legs is very stable.

To recover from sitting, tuck the firing side leg in close and extend the support side leg. Take care not to muzzle your feet or legs.

Roll forward over the firing side leg to a kneeling position. Recover to standing. Remember to maintain your scan as you change levels.

Squat Position

To assume the squat position, disengage the safety and lean forward slightly.

Collapse straight down to the squat position, triceps braced on knees. The soles of the feet should be flat on the ground. The shoulders must be well forward of the hips for recoil management

The elbows move outside of the knees for after action drills.

To recover simply stand up. Remember to continue your scan as you change levels.

Prone Position

Disengage the safety and sink into double kneeling.

Reach out with your support hand as you sprawl forward into prone.

Align the support side elbow directly under the gun. Flatten the feet to minimize motion and reduce your exposure. "Melt into the ground."

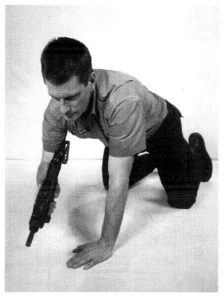

When you decide to rise, bring your support hand back under your chest and push back to double kneeling.

Raise a knee so you have your "get up" foot in place.
Remember to scan at each level.

Harries Flashlight Technique

If you do not have a dedicated light on your weapon, a hand held light can be used. The weapon is supported on the back of the support wrist. The flashlight beam should be aligned with the barrel.

Note that the support forearm is parallel to the ground and the support hand is well clear of the ejection port.

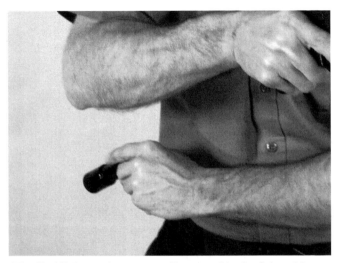

The flashlight can be temporarily stowed in the firing side armpit for reloads and weapon manipulations. Lens should be to the rear in case the light is inadvertently locked on.

Hearing Protection

A low profile, headset type hearing protection with a cutout for a long gun stock is <u>highly</u> recommended, especially if the long gun is your primary home defense weapon. You <u>will</u> lose hearing if you fire a rifle or shotgun inside a closed space with no hearing protection.

High profile, headset type hearing protection may get knocked off the firing side ear. During practice, it is wise to wear an earplug under the firing side earmuff as insurance.

Training Notes

Remember, *no ammunition is used during Dry Practice*!
**Follow the four safety rules and the dry practice
procedures.**

Your two main goals to practice during training for a
potential gunfight are 1) Get the hit and 2) Keep the gun
running.

When practicing techniques, especially new ones, slow is
smooth, and smooth is quick. Be smooth, and you will be
fast when it counts.

Training on a live-fire range will allow you to:

- Safely practice weapons handling with a 'hot' or
  loaded weapon.
- Practice your marksmanship skills.

Some of the drawbacks to range training may be:

- You may be limited in how you move, if not
  required to be completely static.
- You may be on a range that allows you a good field
  of view, especially of your target, and you are
  standing on a firing line in the open with no option
  to seek cover.
- Firing cues are usually commands or the target
  turning towards you, or some other artificial means
  of letting you know it is time to fire.
- You will not get any realistic feedback from your
  target.
- You may be limited in your options on how to
  respond to the threat.
  - You are told how many rounds you may fire,
    and how quickly.
  - You cannot disengage, or back away.

When practicing on your own, as much as possible, you should keep the following in mind:

- Realize that you always have three choices when dealing with an adversary you are not able to avoid, depending on the circumstances:
  - You can hold your ground to see what he does.
  - You can retreat if conditions permit.
  - You can choose to engage if you think it is necessary.
- When dealing with one or more opponents, it is ideal to be in a position of advantage; behind cover or at least concealed from view if at all possible.
- Know how much ambient light is available to you in your environment, and plan accordingly.
  - Master switch for the home that turns on at least one light in every room.
  - Flashlights and spares.
  - Knowing how much light is available to you in case you don't have a master switch or flashlight.
- Is there a way to minimize the threat areas you have to control?
- Is there a way to stack, or line up, multiple threats so they are easier to deal with?
- What in your environment can be used as a barrier to your adversary?

Some questions you need to ask yourself:

- Planning to defend your home is a great idea, but is that the only potential location for an attack on you and your family?

- Have you given thought to a potential fight starting in or around a vehicle or vehicles?

- Have you given serious thought to who you might be fighting? Is it going to be a Hollywood stereotype villain, or are the people you might have to fight going to look like normal, or almost normal, citizens? Are you keeping up with the local news? Who is committing violent crimes in your area, such as armed robbery or home invasions or are involved in carjackings?

- How will you know when to shoot? Have you decided what your 'trigger' or 'line in the sand' is going to be for different situations?

- Once that line is crossed, are you mentally prepared to use deadly force in defense of yourself or others?

- Have you made the decision to be a dedicated opponent? Are you mentally prepared to win, even if you have sustained injuries?

- Have you made decisions on what you should do after the fight?
  - Move to safety.
  - Call for help.
  - Check for and treat any injuries to yourself or family members.
    - o Do you have the training?
    - o Do you have the equipment?
  - Staying busy with planned routines is a good way to blunt the effects of shock and help you stay alert.

Your dry practice should evolve beyond a static firing line, keeping in mind the questions above that pertain to you and your situation. You should practice as much as possible in an appropriate and realistic environment. For example, practicing reloading or clearing malfunctions in a supported position in low light or darkness, actually moving to real or simulated cover, etc. Red guns and Airsoft™ guns are another way to train realistically, where the potential to cover your body or someone else's with a muzzle is heightened.

Sometimes, all you need is your mind and an active imagination in order to practice, at least mentally, what you would do. For example, if you were attacked at a mall, parking garage, traffic light or any public place you and your family might be, how could you avoid or defend?

Remember, YOU are the weapon, your gun is just a tool.

Part Three

In this section:

Reading Your Target

Almost all of your improvement in gun handling and
marksmanship will come through <u>correct</u> dry practice.
However, you must validate that correct dry practice on
occasion with live fire drills. These live fire drills must be
conducted at a proper firing range under carefully controlled
"live fire" conditions.

After firing several bursts to the thoracic cavity of your
target, you will have a group on the target which is full of
valuable information. The diagrams and discussions in this
section will help you diagnose which techniques you are
doing correctly and which ones still need attention. We call
this "Reading Your Target". The following information
assumes your weapon is correctly sighted in and functioning
properly.

You must remember that as the distance to your target
increases small errors in sight alignment, sight picture, and
trigger control that would still allow reasonable hits at close
range will cause peripheral hits or misses.

When firing an automatic weapon, there is a tendency for the shots to spread vertically and to the firing side as the repetitive recoil impulses interact with the firing grip and stance. For this reason, short bursts of two to four rounds are more likely to stay on target than longer bursts.

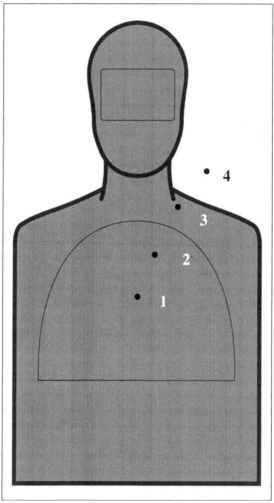

Four round burst illustrating marginal recoil management. Notice that the first two rounds are good hits.

By assuming an effective firing stance with shoulders well forward of the hips, locking the gun firmly into the shoulder pocket, and rolling the elbows in and down, recoil can be managed to control longer bursts.

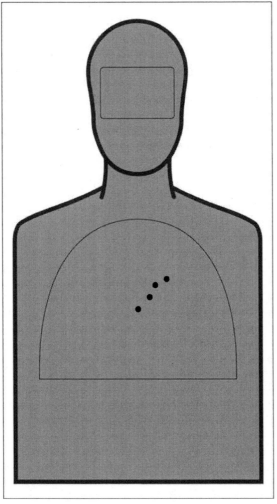

Controlled four round burst in a centered, effective group.

Proper Balance of Speed and Accuracy

Ideally your group will be approximately a hand span in size and well centered in the thoracic cavity. This shows you have the correct balance of speed and accuracy. Remember, under the stress of an actual gunfight, that group will approximately double in size but it will still be inside the thoracic cavity.

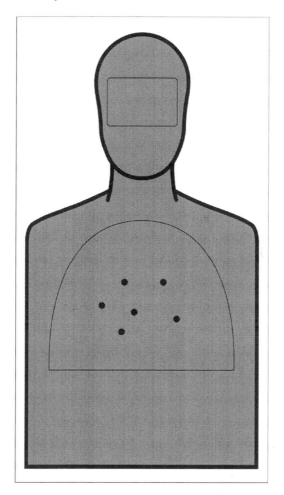

Group Too Small

●

As nice as this group looks, it is too small. You are taking too much time do deliver very accurate shots. On the spectrum of speed vs. accuracy, this group represents too much accuracy. Your opponent may take advantage of your slow delivery and hit you first. Speed up a little bit.

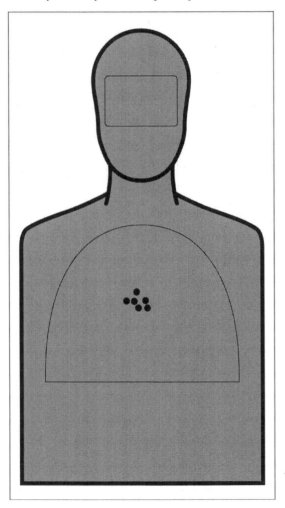

Group Too Large

This group is too large and means you are sacrificing accuracy for speed. You are going too fast. Under the conditions of a gunfight, especially if the range to the target increases, some of these hits will be peripherals or misses. Slow down a little bit.

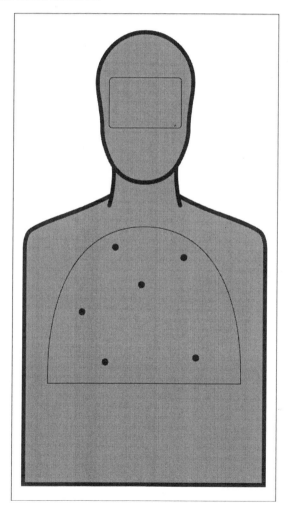

Group Well Centered but Huge

This very large group is indicative of not focusing on the
front sight. You may be looking over the top of the weapon
entirely and focusing on the target or looking through the
sights but focusing at the target. In either case, looking at the
target cannot guarantee proper sight alignment or sight
picture and the hits are poor. Slow down and focus on the
front sight. Depending on the distance to the target, not
focusing on the front sight will cause your shots to miss the
thoracic cavity, if not the target entirely.

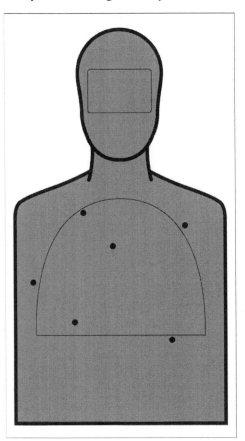

Group High

This is a proper hand span group but it is high in the thoracic cavity. There are two causes for this. First is incorrect sight alignment. You are simply holding the front sight too high in the rear sight. Make certain the front sight tip is centered both vertically and horizontally. Secondly, some shooters aim too high in the thoracic cavity. This is usually caused by a misunderstanding of human anatomy or ballistics of their bullet. Hold right in the center of the thoracic cavity. That gives you the best chance at hitting vital tissue and gives you the largest margin for error.

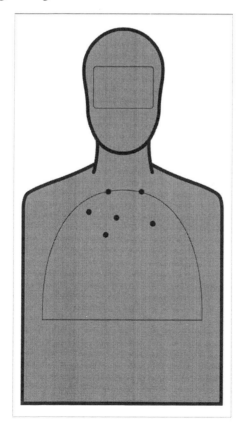

Group Left

Groups which are at the proper height but are off to one side generally reflect incorrect trigger finger placement. If the right-handed shooter is hitting to the left, there is generally not enough trigger finger placed across the face of the trigger. If just the tip of the trigger finger contacts the trigger, the weapon is commonly pushed to the support side as the weapon fires. This can also be caused by a right handed shooter 'bucking' the firing shoulder into the weapon, or a left handed shooter 'flinching' the firing side shoulder away from the weapon, as it is fired in anticipation of the shot being fired and the associated recoil.

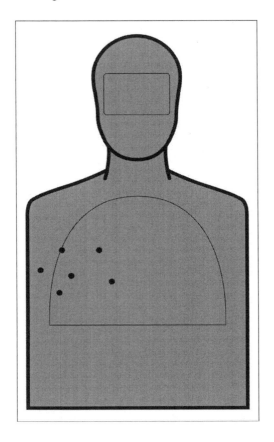

Group Right

If the right-handed shooter is hitting to the right, there is generally too much trigger finger placed across the face of the trigger. The weapon is commonly pulled to the right as the weapon fires. This can also be caused by a left handed shooter 'bucking' the firing shoulder into the weapon, or a right handed shooter 'flinching' the firing side shoulder away from the weapon, as it is fired in anticipation of the shot being fired and the associated recoil.

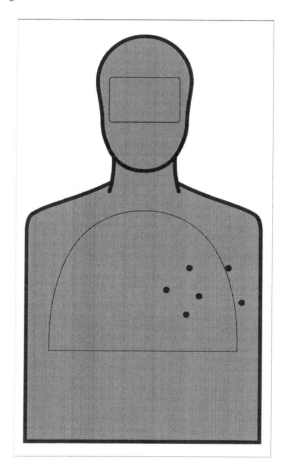

Group Moderately Low

Groups which are near the bottom edge of the thoracic cavity are typically caused by either rushing the trigger press, or at close range, a difference in the sight height over the bore height. Ensure you press the trigger to obtain a surprise break. If it is due to sight height, with a correct zero, you will still be in the thoracic cavity.

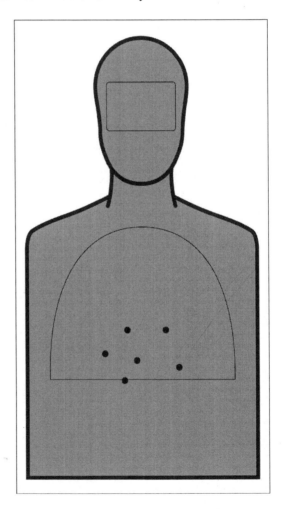

Group Very Low

Groups which are low, or very low and to one side, are caused by "mashing" or "slapping" the trigger. Mashing means squeezing with the whole hand (or hands) just before the shot is fired. Slapping means rushing the trigger press and having the finger fly off the trigger after the shot is fired. Mashing is very easily detected and corrected through dry practice. Mashing is commonly caused by too much shooting and too little dry practice.

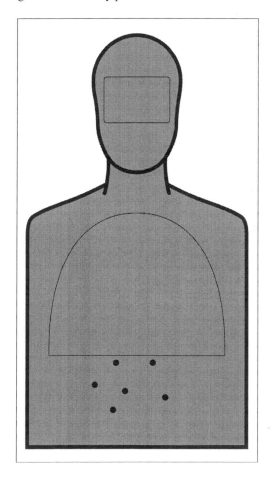

Uzi Skills Test

All shooting is done with selector in full-auto position.

Shooting	Range	Time	Points
Close contact	3m	1.2	15
(Three round burst, once from field ready position)			
Three round burst	3m	1.2	45
(Three times, one from each ready position)			
Two round burst	7 m	1.2	30
(Three times, one from each ready position)			
Two round burst	10 m	1.3	30
(Three times, one from each ready position)			
Two round burst	15 m	1.5	30
(Three times, one from each ready position)			
Two single shots	25 m	2.5	30
(Three times, one from each ready position)			
Two single shots	50 m	3.5	30
(Three times, one from each ready position)			
Single head shot	10 m	1.5	15
(Three times, one from each ready position)			
Hostage rescue	7 m	1.7	30
(Three times each side, one from each ready position)			

Total Points Possible   **255**

Scoring

Each thoracic cavity shot is worth a possible five (5) points
in the thoracic cavity: two (2) points are awarded for all
other areas inside the target silhouette.

Each shot fired beyond the called burst length is minus three
points.

Hostage rescue shots in the cranio-ocular cavity of the hostage taker are worth five (5) points; two (2) points are
awarded for all other areas inside the target silhouette.

Five point penalty for hitting hostage target

Reloads

Penalty points only; assessed for time or procedure violation.
Each reload performed twice.

Description	Time (sec.)	Max. Penalty
Emergency Reload	4.0	-6
Tactical Reload	5.0	-6

Malfunction Clearances

Penalty points only; assessed for time or procedure violation.
Each malfunction clearance performed twice.

Description	Time (sec.)	Max. Penalty
Type 1	1.0	-6
Type 2	1.2	-6
Type 3	5.0	-6

Maximum Points Possible   255

Distinguished Graduate (90%)
Down 26 Points or Less

Graduate (70%)
Down 27-77 Points

Achievement (<70%)
Down 78 points or more

NOTES:

_____

_____

_____

_____

_____

_____

_____

_____

_____

_____

_____

_____

_____

_____

NOTES:

NOTES:

_____

_____

_____

_____

_____

_____

_____

_____

_____

_____

_____

_____

_____

_____

NOTES:

_____

_____

_____

_____

_____

_____

_____

_____

_____

_____

_____

_____

_____

_____

Front Sight Firearms Training Institute
P. O. Box 2619, Aptos, CA 95001
Phone (inside the US): (800) 987-7719
Phone (international): (831) 662-0917
Fax: (831) 684-2137
www.frontsight.com

For more information about Front Sight please email us at
info@frontsight.com

ISBN 0-9711266-4-X